WHO AM I ?
The Story of the Artist

By Serena Bocchino

Revised Edition
Text and illustrations copyright © 2011 by Serena Bocchino.
All rights reserved. Published by **In His Perfect Time** Basking Ridge NJ.

This is the second book of the Am I Collection Series.

ISBN: 978-0-9767674-2-8 (hardcover)
ISBN: 978-0-9767674-9-7 (softcover)
Ebook: 978-0-9767674-7-3 (digital eBook)

Library of Congress Control Number: 2011910609

Designed by Gayle Shimoun
Cover art and illustrations are available as Limited Edition Prints 2011
Distributed by the Am I Collection and Serena Bocchino

No part of this publication may be reproduced or stored in a retrieval system
or transmitted in any form or by any means, electronic, mechanical,
photocopying, recording, or otherwise, without written permission of the publisher/author.

For information regarding permissions or copies of this book, contact:

www.theAmICollection.com
www.serenabocchino.com

Special thanks to designer/artist, Gayle Shimoun for her creativity and fantastic
design sensibility. Her friendship and understanding has been invaluable to this project.

Special thanks to my dearest Stephen, Ezra and Rachel Keough, for their support and inspiration.

Printed in the United States of America

For Rachel Dylan (my daughter) who inspires me always and for Lucia, the artist, (my mom) who taught me and showed me how to be the artist that I am.

I love to draw.

Once I get going, the pictures start flowing.

It can take one little line
and then it grows like a vine.

After drawing, I want to paint.

I combine all different colors, lines and shapes.

I enjoy thinking about
ideas and images that I will use

To create my picture and decide
on the materials I will choose.

I look at the world
and everything around me

Then I imagine and paint it
the way I want it to be.

One thing I know is I love to make things.

I love the joy and satisfaction it brings.

First comes the good feeling it brings to me

Then the wonderful drawings, paintings and sculptures for everyone to see.

I can make some things
big and reach up very high,

Or sometimes I make very small things
and hardly even try.

In the end it is the art-making-act,

That has for me the very greatest impact.

As I get older and learn more about art,

I hope I never lose the exciting part.

I have learned that all artists,
from unknown to great,

have one thing in common when they create.

They express the visual words
that come from their heart,

And this, as you know,
is the most important part.

So when the time comes
when nothing else seems to matter at all,

And I have an idea
that may be great or small,

When I see an image in my mind
that must come out,

I simply know it is from my heart
and that is what it is all about.

Art from the Heart

Fun Art Projects For You to Make

All you will need are crayons, colored pencils, markers or paint.
Choose paper or canvas and the ideas listed below.

Color

The following is a "Color Key" for feelings:
* Red is for feeling Excited.
* Green is for feeling Fresh.
* Blue is for feeling Calm.
* Yellow is for feeling Smart.
* Orange is for feeling Cheerful.
* Purple is for feeling Special.

Create a colorful landscape of how you feel today.

Listen

* Listen to music that you like.
* Close your eyes while you draw or paint what the music sounds like.
* Each time you choose another color or decide to open your eyes you must stop the music until you begin to draw or paint again.

Look

* Look outside your window.
* Everything you see can be created out of shapes.
* Using circles, triangles, squares and rectangles, draw or paint what you see. You may either outline or color in the shapes or do both.
* Remember to use different sizes of these shapes when you are drawing or painting.

Lines

* In your mind, create a musical rhythm such as boom, boom, pow, boom, boom, pow.
* As you think of this rhythm, begin to draw a line that feels and looks like your rhythm.
* For example, you could press hard or soft with your pencil or hardly touch the page at all.
* Create a lot of different rhythms and see what happens after you make 10, 25, or even more lines.
* Use many different colors, types of pencils, markers or crayons.
* Create your own visual music that you can see in your drawing.

Congratulations, you are now a promising young artist!

Serena Bocchino is an artist who visually interprets many different subjects ranging from music to nature to the urban environment. These rhythmic and energectic paintings are an investigation of abstraction and color.

Ms. Bocchino has a Masters Degree from New York University. She has earned awards from many art institutions for her work including New York City's Artists Space, PS1 Contemporary Art Center and the Museum of Modern Art. The New Jersey State Council on the Arts has awarded her fellowships in both painting and drawing. Her work is included in prestigious private, public and corporate collections internationally.

This is Ms. Bocchino's second book in a series about abstract art for children of all ages.

To see additional artwork by the author please visit www.serenabocchino.com.